VINÍCIUS JÚNIOR

VINÍCIUS JÚNIOR

ODYSSEYS

AIDAN WHITCOMB

CREATIVE EDUCATION · CREATIVE PAPERBACKS

Published by Creative Education and Creative Paperbacks
P.O. Box 227, Mankato, Minnesota 56002
Creative Education and Creative Paperbacks are imprints of The Creative Company
www.thecreativecompany.us

Design by Tom Morgan
Art direction by Blue Design, Inc. (www.bluedes.com)

Images by Associated Press/Jose Breton, cover; Dreamstime/Celso Pupo Rodrigues, 16, 19, 20, 26, Cyrnam, 50, Marco Canoniero, 44, Marta Fernndez, 2, 4–5, 6, 11, 56, 59, 62, 64–65, 66, 70–71; Getty Images/Alexander Hassenstein - UEFA, 46, Angel Martinez - Real Madrid, 31, COOLMedia/NurPhoto, 28, FREDERIC J. BROWN , 69, 75, Helios de la Rubia, 37, MARTIN BERNETTI, 12, MAURO PIMENTEL , 24, Mike Egerton - PA Images, 61, Pedro Castillo, 54, Rob Newell - CameraSport, 49, Simon Stacpoole/Offside, 8

Every effort has been made to contact copyright holders for material reproduced in this book. Any omissions will be rectified in subsequent printings if notice is given to the publisher.

Copyright © 2026 Creative Education, Creative Paperbacks
International copyright reserved in all countries. No part of this book may be reproduced in any form without written permission from the publisher.

Library of Congress Cataloging-in-Publication Data
Names: Whitcomb, Aidan author
Title: Vinícius Júnior / by Aidan Whitcomb.
Other titles: Vinícius Jr.
Description: Mankato, Minnesota : Creative Education and Creative Paperbacks, [2026] | Series: Odysseys in sports. Soccer stars | Includes bibliographical references and index. | Audience: Ages 12-15 | Audience: Grades 7-9 | Summary: "Real Madrid forward Vinícius Júnior scored crucial goals in Champions League finals and won the Best FIFA Men's Player award in 2024. Soar along the Brazilian up-and-comer in this action-packed biography for early high school readers"– Provided by publisher.
Identifiers: LCCN 2025012511 (print) | LCCN 2025012512 (ebook) | ISBN 9798895811436 library binding | ISBN 9798896800965 paperback | ISBN 9798895812693 ebook
Subjects: LCSH: Vinícius Júnior, 2000- | Soccer midfielders–Brazil–Biography–Juvenile literature | Soccer players-Brazil-Biography-Juvenile literature | Real Madrid Club de Fútbol-History-Juvenile literature
Classification: LCC GV942.7.V56 W55 2026 (print) | LCC GV942.7.V56 (ebook) | DDC 796.334092 [B]-dc23/eng/20250603
LC record available at https://lccn.loc.gov/2025012511
LC ebook record available at https://lccn.loc.gov/2025012512

Printed in the United States

Vinícius Júnior is known for being one of the most electrifying footballers in the world.

CONTENTS

Introduction 9

Flamengo's Future Star 13
   Brazil's Prodigy 20
   South American Sensation 26

Moving to Madrid 29
   First Trophy with Madrid 37
   A Classic El Clásico 39

Flourishing under Ancelotti 42
   Champions League Glory 49
   Club World Cup Dominance 54

Real Madrid's Front Man 57
   Off-the-Field Impact 70
   Copa América Disaster 75

Selected Bibliography 76

Glossary 77

Websites 79

Index 80

Introduction

It's the 59th minute of the 2022 **UEFA Champions League** (UCL) final. A packed Stade de France hosts two of Europe's greatest clubs, Real Madrid and Liverpool. The back-and-forth match is in a 0–0 stalemate. All of a sudden, Madrid's Federico Valverde bursts down the right side of the pitch, carrying the ball through the Liverpudlian midfield. The midfielder picks up his head to

OPPOSITE: Vinícius Júnior celebrates after scoring Real Madrid's first goal in the 2022 UEFA Champions League final.

survey his options before blasting a low, driven cross toward the back post. In a flash, the young Brazilian speedster Vinícius Júnior slips behind Liverpool's last defender unnoticed. The perfectly placed ball flies past everyone except Vini, who instinctively stretches out his right foot to tap it past the goalie. Real Madrid leads. The Madrid fans who made their way to Paris erupt as Vinícius celebrates, falling to his knees. The Liverpool defenders can only stand frozen. Vinícius has secured Madrid's 14th Champions League title.

Among the world's most electrifying soccer players stands a Brazilian who rose from humble beginnings in the streets of Rio, into a fearless teenager at Flamengo, then the heart of Real Madrid's attack. From the **Campeonato Carioca** to the Champions League, Vinícius has shown why he is one of modern soccer's greats.

Real Madrid celebrates a Champions League win with a parade.

Flamengo's Future Star

Vinícius José Paixão de Oliveira Júnior was born on July 12, 2000, in São Gonçalo, Rio de Janeiro, Brazil. From a young age, Vinícius Júnior knew he wanted to be a soccer star. In 2006, Vinícius's father took the six-year-old to Brazil's biggest club's offices, CR Flamengo, to enroll him into the youth system. The club allowed Vini to join, and he began training with youth team coaches.

OPPOSITE: Vinícius Júnior poses with the best player trophy in the South American U-17 tournament in Rancagua, Chile.

However, there were many obstacles in front of Vinícius. Coming from a poor family, Vinícius struggled getting to the training facilities. He moved in with his uncle, who lived closer to *Ninho do Urubu* (The Vultures' Nest), the youth team headquarters. Vinícius's family also struggled to pay the program's fees. Flamengo graciously aided him financially, seeing his potential.

Despite the challenges, Vinícius became a great young player. His exceptional dribbling, combined with his speed, made him an exciting prospect. Between 2007 and 2010, Vinícius also trained with Flamengo's youth **futsal** team. Futsal coaches loved Vinícius and tried to convince him to pursue futsal. In 2009, Vinícius even completed a trial and was officially invited to join the program. However, Vinícius was adamant—he wanted to play soccer. In 2010, Vinícius had an official tryout with the Flamengo youth team. He was invited to join the youth set-up of Brazil's biggest club. Vinícius was excited to launch his youth career.

At Flamengo, Vinícius quickly stood out among his peers. He could out-dribble, out-run, and out-pass everyone in the academy. Vinícius was Flamengo's prized possession. This recognition also placed pressure on Vinícius. But Vinícius always delivered. His performances at the South American U-15 Championship turned heads across the country. Vinícius carried the momentum into his club competitions. Flamengo officially signed 16-year-old Vinícius as a first team player soon after. Worldwide scouts kept a close eye on his progress. Brazil and especially Flamengo have long been seen as a hotbed of talent. Legendary players like Zico and Adriano had

Vini reacts during a heated match.

come through the academy before him and made it big in Europe. Vinícius hoped to follow in their footsteps.

Vini had another great tournament with Brazil at the 2017 South American U-17 Championship. In two youth international tournaments, Vinícius cemented himself as a star in the making. Many teams were intrigued by the idea of signing Vinícius, but he would command a hefty price.

In Vinícius's first season with the first team, he appeared in 37 games. Before Vinícius joined the senior squad in May, Flamengo breezed through their domestic league, the Campeonato Carioca. The team defeated rivals Fluminense 3–1 on aggregate in a tense final. Soon after, on May 13, 2017, Vinícius made his professional debut, subbing into a **Campeonato Brasileiro Série A** game against Atlético Mineiro. Two days later, Vinícius signed a contract extension with Flamengo. The new contract increased his release clause to around $53 million. The move paved the way for Spanish giants Real Madrid to swoop in and make a record-breaking purchase.

On May 23, Real Madrid activated the release clause and signed Vinícius. At the time, the move was the second-most expensive transfer fee for a player from the Brazilian league, behind Neymar. It was also the most expensive transfer for a player under 19 years old. As Vinícius was only 16, he wasn't allowed to make an international transfer until he turned 18. He remained with Flamengo, on loan from Madrid, until the 2018–19 Spanish season.

Vinícius was determined to make the most of his remaining time in Brazil. Flamengo carried their success from the Carioca into their other competitions. In

The young Vini displayed exceptional dribbling skills.

Brazil's Prodigy

Vinícius's first chance to showcase his talents to a global audience was with Brazil at the 2015 South American U-15 Championship. Vini and Brazil rolled through the tournament. After defeating Chile 3–2 in the opener, he scored his first goal against Peru in a 6–1 thrashing. He tallied two more goals against Bolivia and one against Uruguay. Brazil topped their group. In the semifinals, Vinícius's double led Brazil to a 3–1 victory over Ecuador. The scoreless final went to a penalty shootout, but the Brazilians edged Uruguay for their record fourth title. For his efforts, Vinícius was named Player of the Tournament.

a competitive Série A, Flamengo finished sixth, qualifying them for the **Copa Libertadores**. Vinícius logged 25 appearances in the Brasileiro, scoring three goals and adding an assist. That first assist came against Ponte Preta, when Vinícius's perfectly weighted cross found Leandro Damião's head to score the game's second goal.

As the season progressed, Vinícius saw more playing time. In a **Copa Sudamericana** match against Chile's Palestino, Vinícius scored his first professional goal. A minute after subbing in, Vinícius pounced on his teammate's missed header to make the score 5–0. Soon after, in a Brasileiro match against Atlético Goianiense, Vinícius scored both goals in a 2–0 win, showcasing his blistering pace in each.

Flamengo's best competition was the Sudamericana. Vinícius played in seven matches, injecting energy off the bench. After advancing past Palestino 10–2 on aggregate, Flamengo knocked Chapecoense out in the round of 16. In a pair of classic Fla-Flu **derby** matches, Flamengo defeated Fluminense 4–3 in the quarterfinals. A victory over Colombia's Atlético Junior in the semifinals sent Flamengo to their first ever Copa Sudamericana finals appearance against Argentina's Independiente. Vinícius featured in both matches. Unfortunately, Flamengo's run would end there, as Independiente were crowned champions. Vinícius would have to wait for his first continental club trophy. Vinícius played sparingly in Flamengo's other competitions, including the **Copa do Brasil**, finishing as runners-up to Cruzeiro. Throughout, Vini showed glimpses of stardom in his first year in professional soccer. The sky would be the limit in Madrid.

In Vinícius's final half season in Brazil, he transitioned from a promising prospect to an elite player for Flamengo. Vinícius benefited from new managers Paulo César Carpegiani and Mauricio Barbieri, who were more willing to let their youngster shine, before he headed off to Europe. Vinícius grew in confidence, developing into one of the best attacking players in Brazil at just 17.

In the Carioca, Vinícius made 12 appearances, leading Flamengo with four goals. Flamengo made quick work of the first stage, winning six of seven matches. In the secondary stage, they had a few stumbles,

Vini made key contributions in club competitions in Brazil.

including a 0–4 loss to Fluminense. Still, Flamengo advanced to the Carioca's final stage but were shockingly eliminated by the eventual champions Botafogo.

Vinícius also made contributions in the other club competitions. He started in both round-of-16 matches in the Copa do Brasil, with Flamengo narrowly avoiding an upset by Ponte Preta, winning 1–0 on aggregate. Vini also appeared five times in the Copa Libertadores. His signature moment of the competition came against Ecuadorian side Emelec. After going down 0–1 in the 65th minute, Vinícius scored twice in seven minutes. For the first goal, Vinícius weaved through three defenders and blasted a shot into the roof of the net. The winner was another spectacular effort, finishing off a counterattack with a left-footed curler past an outstretched keeper.

South American Sensation

At the 2017 South American U-17 Championship, Vinícius again shone on the international stage. The Brazilians dominated the competition. In their first game against Peru, Vinícius opened the scoring, sliding a left-footed shot past the goalkeeper. Brazil would win 3-0. After beating Venezuela, Vinícius scored the only Brazilian goal in a 1-1 draw with Paraguay. Brazil topped rivals Argentina, and Vinícius added to his goal tally in wins against Venezuela again, Ecuador, and Colombia. Brazil routed Chile 5-0 in the final to clinch their 12th title. Vinícius's seven

In the Brasileiro, Vinícius played 12 matches, starting 11 of them. He added another four goals to his season total. Flamengo was in first for the majority of the time Vinícius was in Brazil but finished as runners-up after he left. Vinícius finished with 10 goals and 4 assists in the 2018 season.

His final match in red and black came in a tough 1–1 draw against Palmeiras. After the match, Vinícius was emotional. His short but productive time in Brazil had come to a close. Many begged for him to stay and try to win the league, but it was time to leave. The allure of Real Madrid was too much, and Vinícius was excited to further his career. In 1.5 years in Flamengo's first team, Vinícius made 69 appearances and scored 14 goals.

Moving to Madrid

Vinícius was officially presented as a Real Madrid player on July 20, 2018. Vinícius was initially assigned to Real Madrid Castilla, the reserve team, to gradually adapt to the European style. But he exceeded all expectations. Vinícius dominated the Segunda División B, amassing four goals in five matches. In his second game, against Atlético Madrid B, Vinícius scored twice. He was ready to take the next step.

OPPOSITE: Having moved to Real Madrid, Vini quickly adapted to the European style of play.

On September 29, 2018, first team manager Julen Lopetegui called up Vinícius for a **La Liga** match against Atlético Madrid. In the 87th minute, Vini made his Real Madrid debut, subbing into the scoreless match. Soon after, Vinícius cemented himself in the first team. However, with Madrid having a slow start, Lopetegui was fired. Santiago Solari took over, and in Solari's first La Liga match, against Real Valladolid, Vinícius scored his first Madrid goal. The teenager fired a shot that took a massive deflection past Valladolid's goalkeeper. It wasn't the prettiest, but it ignited the **Bernabéu**. Eighteen-year-old Vinícius became the sixth-youngest goal scorer in Real Madrid history, and the youngest foreign scorer.

Vinícius's best competition was the **Copa del Rey**. He received extended minutes, growing his confidence. Vini started all of Madrid's matches and contributed two goals and seven assists. In the round of 32 **legs** against UD Melia, Vinícius had a stand-out performance providing three assists and a goal. Vinícius continued to make goal contributions in the round of 16 and the quarterfinals,

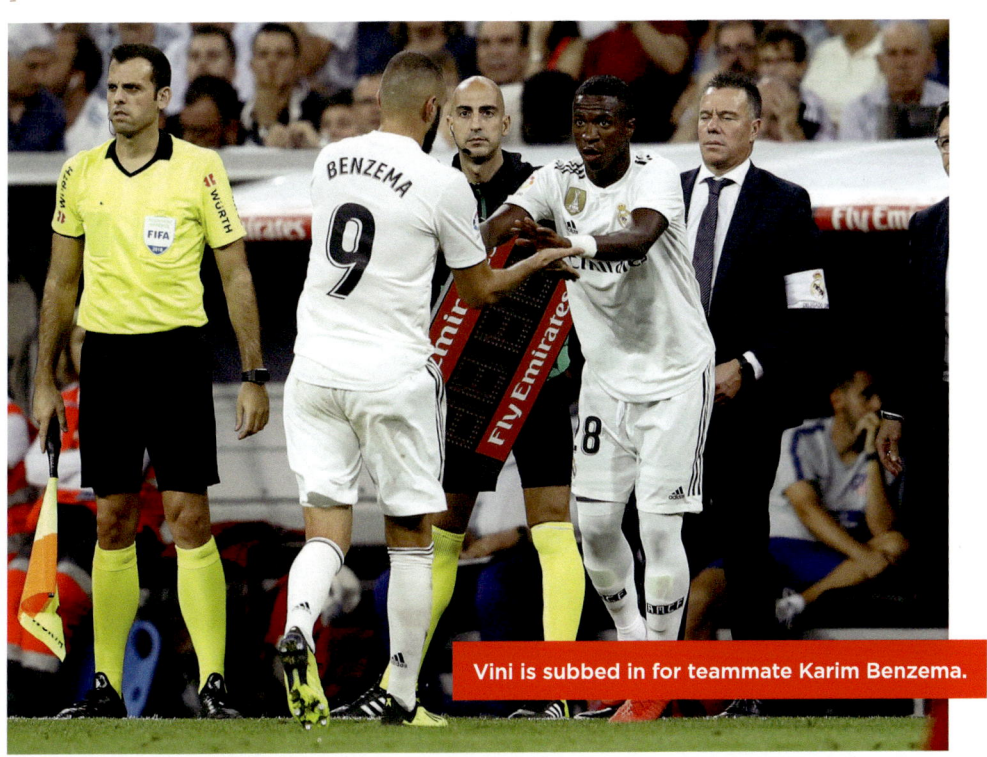

Vini is subbed in for teammate Karim Benzema.

before meeting Barcelona in the semifinals. After a 1–1 draw in the first leg, Madrid couldn't keep their run alive, losing 0–3 in the second.

Vinícius got his first taste of the Champions League as well. In his first appearance, Vini assisted Toni Kroos in a 5–0 win over Viktoria Plzeň. Madrid advanced into the knockouts, where they would face tournament dark horses Ajax. Things looked good for the defending champs in the first leg, as Real Madrid won 2–1 on the road. Vinícius assisted Karim Benzema's opening goal, dancing around the Dutch team's defense. However, in the second leg, Real Madrid were shockingly eliminated, falling 1–4 at home. Vinícius would also suffer a ligament injury. The injury held him out for much of the rest of the season.

Real Madrid had a relatively poor season by their standards. They did win the 2018 **Club World Cup**, but Madrid only mustered third in La Liga, well behind champions Barcelona. However, a positive was the return of manager Zinedine Zidane in March. In total, Vinícius played 31 matches in his debut season, scoring four times. While the injury did put an abrupt end to a solid season, Vinícius showed glimpses of future stardom.

After Brazilian manager Tite decided to not take Vinícius to the 2019 **Copa América**, which Brazil won, Vinícius entered the 2019–20 season on a mission.

However, he faced stiff competition for minutes in a talented squad. Players like Eden Hazard and Benzema had more experience, and Zidane leaned on them early. Still, Zidane gave Vinícius plenty of opportunities. One of Zidane's favorite substitutes, Vinícius often impacted matches against tired defenders, utilizing his special speed. In La Liga, Vinícius scored three goals in 29 matches. Real Madrid and Barcelona traded blows all season. However, after La Liga returned from a three-month hiatus due to the COVID-19 pandemic, Madrid pulled away en route to a 34th league title.

Vinícius also appeared in other competitions. In the **Supercopa de España** final against Atlético Madrid, Vinícius subbed late into the goalless match, helping through extra time. Real were crowned champions after a penalty shootout. That same success wasn't found in the Copa del Rey. Vinícius did score in a round-of-16 win against Real Zaragoza, but Real were eliminated in the following match by Real Sociedad.

Real Madrid had another poor Champions League year. The team limped through the group stage. An opening 0–3 loss to Paris Saint-Germain (PSG) and two more draws were unexpected. In the group finale, against Belgium's Club Brugge, Vinícius was handed a start. Vinícius was lively, and in the 64th-minute of a 1–1 game, he got Madrid the lead, poking home a loose ball for his first Champions League goal. Madrid made the knockouts and had to play Manchester City. Zidane again started Vinícius, and it paid dividends. Vinícius assisted Isco before subbing out. Then, Madrid began to crumble. They conceded twice in the final 15 minutes and were stunned at home. After returning in August from the COVID interruption, Manchester City advanced past Vinícius and Real Madrid. In total, Vinícius scored five goals and assisted three times in the 2019–20 season. Zidane was cautious with his minutes but still used him to affect games. Vinícius took on more responsibilities as the season progressed, and the future looked bright.

The COVID interruption meant the 2020–21 season arrived quickly. Vinícius took advantage of Hazard's inconsistencies and injuries, securing a larger role. He finished with 48 total appearances, 6 goals, and 4 assists.

First Trophy with Madrid

One unique competition Vinícius had the chance to participate in was the 2018 **FIFA** Club World Cup. Real Madrid had qualified, having won the previous season's UEFA Champions League. Vinícius didn't play in the semifinal victory over Japan's Kashima Antlers, but did sub into the final against the United Arab Emirates' Al-Ain. Vinícius created the final goal in the 4–1 win, dribbling through a tired Al-Ain backline before poking a shot that deflected in off a defender. The Club World Cup was the first trophy Vinícius lifted with Real Madrid.

In La Liga, Vinícius started strongly, scoring in back-to-back matches against Real Valladolid and Levante. The season was a three-way title fight with Real, Atlético, and Barcelona neck-and-neck throughout the year. Real Madrid did well against their closest rivals, winning both **Clásico** matches and taking four points off Atlético. But disappointing losses to mid-table clubs ultimately spoiled their chances, and they finished two points behind Atlético. Vinícius's three goals and three assists showed continual improvement.

Real Madrid's disappointment was compounded in the two domestic tournaments. In the Supercopa, Real Madrid were eliminated in the semifinals. A week later in the Copa del Rey, Real Madrid suffered a shocking defeat. Third-division side Alcoyano pulled off a historic upset. After equalizing in the 80th minute, Vinícius was

A Classic El Clásico

Vini's best game of the 2019–20 La Liga campaign came in the March El Clásico against Barcelona. In the 71st minute, Vinícius snuck behind Barcelona's backline, received a pass from Toni Kroos, and beat the goalie Marc-André ter Stegen at his near post. The Bernabéu erupted as their youngster gave Real the lead. Madrid would go on to win 2–0, and 19-year-old Vinícius became the youngest Real Madrid player to score in El Clásico in the 21st century. The win was crucial to Real Madrid, with the two sides locked in a tightly contested title race.

replaced by Marco Asensio. In extra time, Alcoyano, reduced to 10 men, pushed forward and scored a famous winner to knock out the giants.

Vinícius broke through during the Champions League competition. He began as an impact substitute, with a goal in the group opener against Shakhtar

Donetsk seconds after coming on. The winger surprised Shakhtar's center back, cleanly picking his pocket before scoring. Real Madrid advanced as group winners, setting up a round-of-16 tie with Serie A's Atalanta. After breezing through the Italian side 4–1, Vinícius had his best performance in the quarterfinals against Liverpool. In Madrid, Vinícius opened the scoring, settling a perfect Kroos long ball with his chest, bursting through the defense, and sliding past goalkeeper Alisson. In the second half, Vinícius's sharp first-time finish gave Real a 3–1 advantage. Madrid fans around the world praised Vinícius's breakout game. Unfortunately, the UCL run would end in the next round as eventual champions Chelsea eliminated them 3–1 on aggregate. Although the season was trophy-less, Vinícius performed well, becoming a regular starter at just 20 years old.

"ANCELOTTI WAS CONFIDENT HE COULD BRING MADRID BACK TO TROPHY-WINNING WAYS."

In the summer, Vini was disappointed to not be a major part of Brazil's Copa America 2021 team. Brazil would finish runners-up, but he only made four brief substitute appearances. Vinícius used the remainder of the summer to rest. With Zidane stepping down, Carlo Ancelotti was named new manager of Real Madrid. He was confident he could bring Madrid back to trophy-winning ways. Ancelotti also believed in his talented youngster, promising to unlock the most of his potential.

Flourishing under Ancelotti

With Hazard still struggling to stay healthy, Vinícius took Madrid's starting left winger job. Under Ancelotti, Vinícius flourished. He soared past career highs in goals and assists.

Vini started the 2021–22 season hot, scoring five goals and adding three assists in his first six games. Against Valencia, Vinícius sparked a dramatic comeback, scoring in the 86th minute to tie and assisting Benzema's winner in the 88th. Against Sevilla, Vinícius's 87th-minute rocket handed the team an important 2–1 victory. The win secured Madrid's place atop the table, and they never looked back. Vinícius racked up the goals and assists as Madrid cruised. Against Levante in May, Vinícius tallied his first La Liga hat-trick. He also assisted in a 6–0 romp. By the season's end, Vinícius contributed to Madrid's 13-point La Liga victory with 17 goals and 13 assists. He finished third in La Liga in goals and assists. Vinícius also helped in the Copa del Rey and Supercopa, with Madrid winning the latter. Vinícius was no longer just an exciting young prospect, but an established superstar.

But it was in the Champions League that Vinícius dazzled. Real Madrid coasted through their group. Despite a stunning 1–2 loss to Moldova's Sheriff Tiraspol,

Vini in Champions League play

Madrid won their other five contests, conceding only once. Vinícius scored twice and assisted three times. In the round of 16, Madrid faced PSG. After a 0–1 first leg loss, Madrid bounced back to win 3–1 to advance. Next, Madrid faced an English gauntlet. In the quarterfinals, Real Madrid played defending champs Chelsea. A Benzema hat-trick in London gave Real a massive advantage. However, the Blues stormed into the Bernabéu with a blistering start, leading 3–0 by the 75th minute. For a moment, Chelsea was through on aggregate. Then, in the 80th minute, Rodrygo leveled the tie to go to extra time. In extra time, Vinícius's poked cross towards Benzema was headed past the Chelsea goalkeeper to save Madrid's campaign.

Man City and Madrid provided another entertaining tie in the semifinals. The first leg was a wild 4–3

win for the English side, with Vinícius scoring once. Again, Real Madrid needed a comeback. In one of the UCL's craziest games, Madrid entered the 90th minute down 3–5 on aggregate. However, two goals within a minute by Rodrygo again got Madrid into extra time.

OPPOSITE Vini scores Real Madrid's winning goal in the 2022 Champions League final against Liverpool.

In extra time, a Benzema penalty kick brought Madrid to another final.

The Champions League Final between Real Madrid and Liverpool was another classic between two of Europe's most successful clubs. The game was a tight back-and-forth, but neither side could find the goal. Then, up stepped Vini. Vini's goal in the second half was all it took to beat Liverpool 1–0. Madrid were champions of Europe again. In the biggest match of his life, Vinícius delivered, becoming one of the youngest UCL final goal scorers. He was named Champions League Young Player of the Season.

Vinícius finished the season with 22 goals and 19 assists, logging more than 4,000 minutes. In March, Vinícius also scored his first goal for Brazil. In a FIFA World Cup qualifier against Chile, Vinícius scored in front of a lively

Maracanã crowd. Many of those same fans had watched Vinícius as a Flamengo prodigy. The following summer, he settled in with the national team. In a pair of June **friendlies** against South Korea and Japan, he performed well, locking down a starting job.

Vinícius continued his strong play into 2022–23. Ancelotti remained the manager, hoping to win more trophies in six competitions. Starting with the UEFA Super Cup against Europa League champions Eintracht Frankfurt, Real Madrid controlled the match to lift their fifth Cup. Vinícius's assist to Benzema sealed the 2–0 victory. The team had good starts in the other campaigns, too. In La Liga, Real Madrid started 12 games undefeated. In those 12 games, Vinícius scored six and assisted three goals. Real also performed well in the Champions League group stage. Vinícius scored

Champions League Glory

The 2022 UCL final was a rematch of the 1981 and 2018 finals between Real Madrid and Liverpool, with each club winning once. In the biggest match of his career, Vinícius was a constant threat, troubling the Liverpool backline with his pace. After a scoreless first half, the breakthrough came in the 59th minute. Timing his run perfectly, Vinícius got behind the defense to receive a perfect Federico Valverde cross at the back post and coolly scored, giving Madrid a 1–0 lead. Despite a flurry of late Liverpool chances, Madrid goalie Thibaut Courtois stood tall, keeping a clean sheet. As the final whistle sounded, Vinícius and his teammates celebrated their record-extending 14th UCL title.

in four of their matches as Madrid topped their group. Vinícius's success was being recognized globally. In October, he finished eighth in the 2022 Ballon d'Or voting. Vini was flying as the World Cup tournament interrupted the season.

At the 2022 Qatar World Cup, Vinícius was Brazil's starting left winger. There was pressure on Brazil to perform well after failed recent tournaments. Most pressure fell on veterans like Neymar, but there were expectations on Vini, too. In the opener, Brazil battled Serbia hard to a 2–0 victory. Vinícius was key to both goals. The first was created off a Vinícius shot parried into Richarlison, who poked the ball into the net. Then, Vinícius assisted Richarlison's second with an outside-of-the boot cross, which was stunningly bicycle-kicked into the net. Against Switzerland, Vinícius had a goal disallowed, but Casemiro's late volley broke the deadlock as Brazil won 1–0. The win qualified them to the round of 16.

Vinícius's best game came against South Korea. In a dominant Brazil performance, Vinícius started the party in the seventh minute, scoring his first World Cup goal. His calm finish was celebrated by the first of four Brazilian samba parties. Vinícius assisted Brazil's fourth goal with a clever cross to Lucas Paqueta. Brazil won 4–1 and immediately became a tournament favorite. However, just as Brazil hit their peak, their cup dreams were dashed by Croatia. The underdogs upset Brazil on penalties in the quarterfinals, and Brazil's World Cup drought continued.

Back with Madrid, Vinícius continued his conquest through six competitions in the Spanish Supercopa. After squeaking past Valencia, Madrid weren't able to win an El Clásico final. Barcelona dominated their rivals

3–1. They were able to win the Club World Cup for the season's second trophy. Real Madrid also won the Copa del Rey. In the run, Vini tallied three goals and three assists. His best game came against Barcelona. Despite losing the home leg 0–1, Madrid rolled their rivals at Camp Nou, winning 4–0. Vinícius scored the first just before halftime and drew the penalty for Madrid's third. He assisted Benzema's hat-trick to complete the rout. Vinícius lifted Madrid's third trophy a month later in a 2–1 win over Osasuna, assisting the game's opening goal.

Real Madrid faltered a bit in the second half of the season. In La Liga, a rough spring allowed Barcelona to coast to a 10-point win. Vinícius's 10 goals and 9 assists in the league were only a consolation. Likewise, the quest for back-to-back Champions League titles blew up in the semifinals. The knockouts started well. The round-of-16

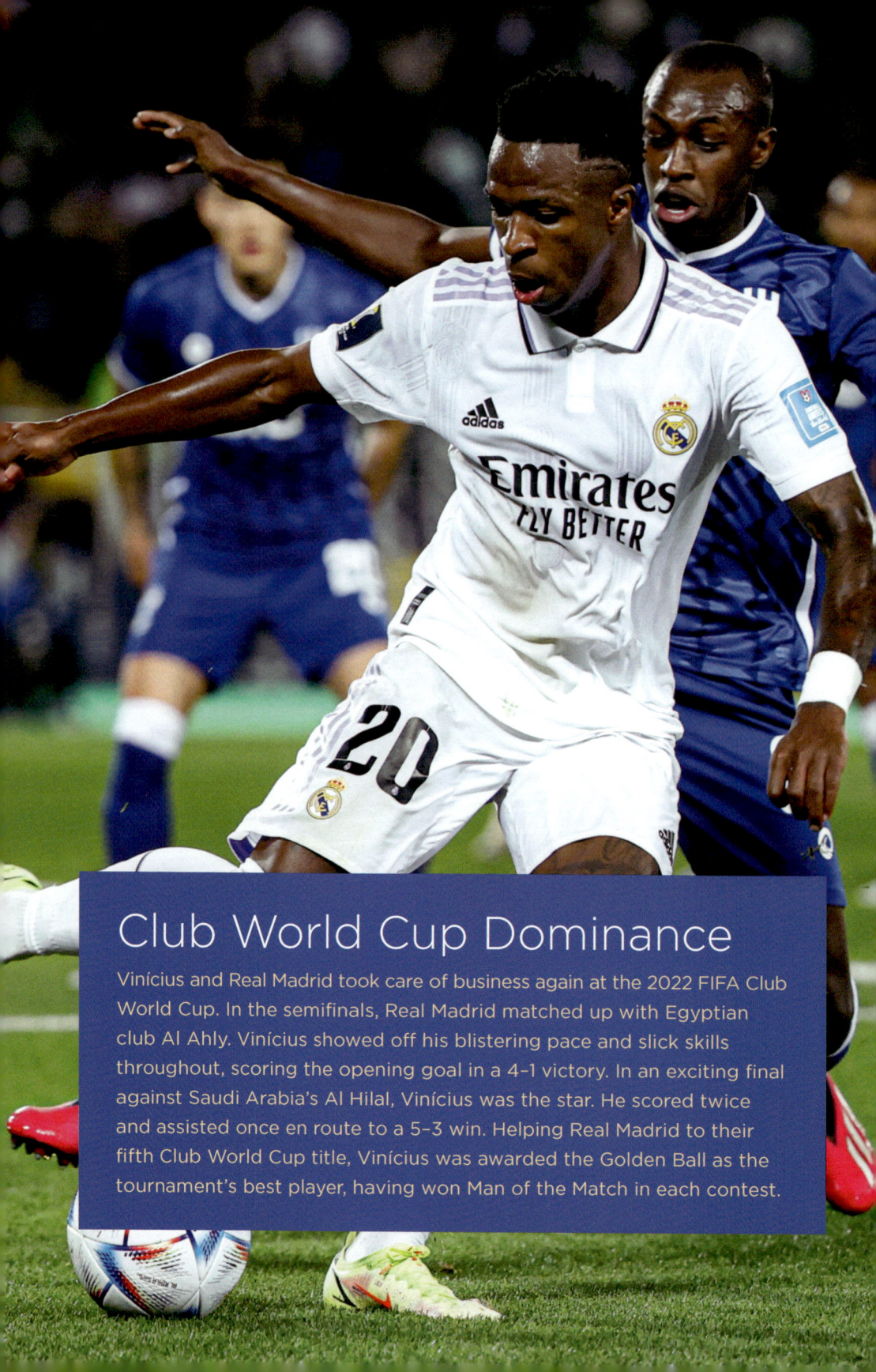

Club World Cup Dominance

Vinícius and Real Madrid took care of business again at the 2022 FIFA Club World Cup. In the semifinals, Real Madrid matched up with Egyptian club Al Ahly. Vinícius showed off his blistering pace and slick skills throughout, scoring the opening goal in a 4-1 victory. In an exciting final against Saudi Arabia's Al Hilal, Vinícius was the star. He scored twice and assisted once en route to a 5-3 win. Helping Real Madrid to their fifth Club World Cup title, Vinícius was awarded the Golden Ball as the tournament's best player, having won Man of the Match in each contest.

tie was a previous year's final rematch against Liverpool. Down 0–2 in the first leg, Madrid scored six unanswered between the legs. Vinícius scored twice and assisted twice. Madrid won a pair of 2–0 games against Chelsea in the quarterfinals to face Man City in the semifinals. After a tightly contested 1–1 draw, where Vinícius scored a rocket, Madrid was blanked 0–4 in the second leg. Still, Vini landed on the UCL Team of the Tournament, having supplied seven goals and five assists.

A trio of trophies, multiple individual honors, plus 23 goals and 18 assists, proved that Vinícius was one of the world's best. He was the most influential player on one of the world's biggest teams. As a reward, Vinícius was handed Madrid's iconic number 7 jersey, worn by legends like Cristiano Ronaldo and Raul. Vinícius would face a new type of pressure entering 2023–24 as the face of Real Madrid.

VINÍCIUS JÚNIOR

Real Madrid's Front Man

In his first season as Real Madrid's front man, Vini delivered standout performances, key to their incredible year. Madrid lost just one game in regulation all season, and none when Vinícius was on the field. The only thing slowing Vinícius down was the first real injury problems of his career. He missed 11 matches between the Champions League and La Liga due to a pair of leg muscle injuries.

OPPOSITE: Vini leads Real Madrid in a 2024 match against Atlético Madrid.

In 26 La Liga appearances, Vinícius scored 15 goals and provided five assists. He only scored four league goals before New Year's, but that relatively slow start was mostly due to injuries. Still, Vinícius was rewarded for his stellar play. On October 30, Vinícius finished sixth in the 2023 Ballon d'Or voting. The next day, Real Madrid announced a contract extension until 2027. Vinícius wanted to continue in the capital through his prime.

One of Vinícius's best games in La Liga came against Valencia in March. Down 0–2 early, Vinícius willed his team to preserve what would be a 32-game unbeaten streak with a pair of goals. With three goals and an assist in the next two games, Vini put together a fantastic March, winning the La Liga Player of the Month. In the end, Vinícius and Real Madrid breezed through La Liga, winning by 10 points and amassing a 61-goal differential.

Vini made the La Liga Team of the Season in 2024.

Madrid had the best attack in the league, spearheaded by Vinícius and newcomer Jude Bellingham, and the best defense. Both Bellingham and Vini were named to the La Liga Team of the Season.

Another trophy was won in the Supercopa, defeating Barcelona in the final. Vini's first-half hat-trick against his rivals carried Madrid to a 4–1 victory. Vinícius became the first Brazilian to score three times for Madrid against Barcelona. Vini's combination of pace and precision, with all the talent around him, made Real Madrid likely the best team in the world.

Real Madrid and Vinícius again found success in the Champions League. Injuries limited Vinícius to three group stage appearances, but he did score twice and assist three times. Vinícius was healthy and at his best in the knockouts. In the round of 16, Real Madrid navigated a tricky draw against RB Leipzig. Vinícius scored Madrid's only goal in the second leg, using a clever run to get just enough space for Bellingham to find him, before lashing the ball into the net. A mammoth quarterfinals matchup with Man City went all the way to penalties. In a thrilling 3–3 first leg draw, Vinícius assisted twice, including Valverde's 79th-minute equalizer. The second

Real Madrid vs. Man City

Vini led Real Madrid to success in the 2024 Champions League.

leg also finished 1–1 after regulation. A scoreless extra time brought the game to penalties, where the Spanish team edged out their opponents.

Vinícius's best game of the tournament came in the first leg semifinal against Bayern Munich. Bayern controlled much of the game, but Vinícius's speed was a constant threat. That speed was unleashed to score the opener in the 24th minute, and a late penalty gave the forward his brace as Madrid escaped Munich with a 2–2 draw. Vinícius scored in the UCL semifinals for a third consecutive season. However, back home, Madrid was on the brink of elimination, down 0–1 late on. But an unlikely hero emerged to snatch a famous victory when Joselu scored twice in the 88th and 91st minutes. The effort drew comparisons to Rodrygo's improbable double

Vini sports Real Madrid's orange jersey, officially unveiled in 2024–25.

two years earlier. Once more, Vinícius was back in the UCL final.

In the title match, Real Madrid faced unlikely finalists Borussia Dortmund. The game was tense, with both sides unable to find a goal. Dortmund had many chances, but finally the more experienced team showed their Eu-

> **OPPOSITE** Real Madrid celebrate their 36th league title in 2024.

ropean prowess. Through Dani Carvajal, Madrid took the lead in the 74th minute. Vinícius got his goal eight minutes later, sealing the victory. With his goal, Vinícius became the youngest player to score in two UCL finals, beating Lionel Messi's record. Vinícius also won UCL Player of the Season for his six-goal, five-assist tournament. Across 2023–24, Vinícius racked up 24 goals and 10 assists, playing in just 39 matches.

Vinícius served as captain of Brazil for the first time in a friendly against Spain on March 26, 2024. The match was played at the Bernabéu and ended in an exciting 3–3 draw. But Vini's most important time with the national team came at the summer's Copa América 2024 tournament. There was a lot of pressure on Vini to lead Brazil to a trophy. Unfortunately, almost everything went wrong. The team limped through the group stage, and Vinícius received a suspension for yellow card accumulation, holding him out of their knockout game. Missing their key player, Brazil were flat, and sent packing. It was another tournament without a trophy. The inability to capitalize on their country's talent infuriated fans. They were upset at the team and Vinícius. Vinícius apologized for his suspension, regretting his actions. He would have to wait until the 2026 World Cup for another major international trophy chance.

Things started well for Vinícius in the 2024–25 season. Real Madrid added another star forward, signing sensation Kylian Mbappé. The Mbappé, Vini, and Bellingham attack was among the greatest trios of the decade. With the newly created FIFA Intercontinental Cup and the reworked Club World Cup, Madrid would compete for seven trophies. Vinícius and Madrid lifted their first

Copa América 2024

Off-the-Field Impact

On the same day that Vinícius finished sixth in the 2023 Ballon d'Or voting, he was also honored as the recipient of the Sócrates Award. The award recognizes a player who makes significant contributions to social or humanitarian causes worldwide. The award committee honored Vinícius's efforts fighting against racism and his work with the Instituto Vini Jr. With his organization, Vinícius works to improve conditions in Brazilian public schools with better technology and additional teaching resources. The award was a great achievement for Vinícius, highlighting his impact both on and off the field.

in the UEFA Super Cup. Real defeated 2023–24 Europa League winners Atalanta 2–0, with Vinícius assisting the opening goal, skipping past defenders to set up Valverde. He also helped Madrid win the Intercontinental Cup, beating Mexican side Pachuca 3–0 in the final. Vinícius assisted Mbappé's opener and scored a penalty. Real, however, did not win the Supercopa, losing to Barcelona 2–5 in the final. Vinícius was a consistent performer, with many of his best performances coming in the new Champions League group stage format. Vinícius scored seven goals in six games. In the 5–2 win against Dortmund, Vinícius scored his first hat-trick in a European competition.

The only disappointment for Vinícius was the result of the 2024 Ballon d'Or. After his incredible 2023–24 season, many believed Vinícius would win the award. His

"REAL MADRID AND VINÍCIUS BOYCOTTED THE CEREMONY IN PROTEST OF WHAT THEY THOUGHT WAS AN UNFAIR DECISION."

Champions League heroics and his team's success made him a prime candidate for his first Ballon d'Or. However, it was Manchester City's Rodri who won. The decision was controversial. Real Madrid and Vinícius boycotted the ceremony in protest of what they thought was an unfair decision. There were mixed reactions. Some called out the ceremony for disrespecting Madrid and Vinícius.

Some saw the snub as retaliation for Vinícius's history of calling out racism. Others were upset with Madrid, saying that the boycott was disrespectful and petty.

Even without the Ballon d'Or, Vinícius is one of his generation's greats. From his early days at Flamengo to becoming a key player at Real Madrid, Vinícius has wowed and inspired millions. His electric speed, skillful dribbling, and clutch performances have made him a nightmare to face. He carries the hopes of a soccer-crazed country, eager to win trophies once again. However, Vinícius's story is still being written. Will he get revenge and win a Ballon d'Or? Can he lead Brazil to a first World Cup victory since 2002? No matter what's in store, Vinícius's journey has been full of unforgettable moments, and the best might be yet to come.

Copa América Disaster

Brazil was among the favorites at Copa América 2024, and fans were getting anxious about winning another international trophy. Manager Dorival Junior's squad, mixed with veterans and talents, was led by Vinícius. After a frustrating 0–0 draw against Costa Rica in the opener, Vini's brace in a 4–1 win against Paraguay changed the mood of Brazilian fans. However, a disaster match against Colombia proved costly. Not only was Brazil held to a draw, but Vinícius picked up a second yellow card of the tournament, meaning he would be suspended for the knockout match against Uruguay. Brazil lacked Vinícius's cutting edge, falling in penalty kicks to their South American rivals.

Selected Bibliography

Cortegana, Mario. "Mbappe, Vinicius Jr and Bellingham: Real Madrid's third wave of 'galacticos' are just getting started." *The Athletic,* 2024, https://www.nytimes.com/athletic/6015731/2024/12/29/mbappe-vinicius-bellingham-real-madrid-mvb/

Geoffreys, Clayton. *Vinicius Junior: The Inspiring Story of One of Soccer's Star Forwards*. Independently published, 2024.

Goldblatt, David. *Futebol Nation: The Story of Brazil Through Soccer*. Bold Type Books, 2014.

Kirkland, Alex and Tim Vickery. "Vinícius is a star at Real Madrid, but why not for Brazil?" *ESPN,* 2024, https://www.espn.com/soccer/story/_/id/42348422/vinicius-junior-star-real- madrid-why-not-brazil

Mallow, Max. "Baila Vini! Real Madrid's Vinicius Junior Danced to His Own Tune in 2024." *Sports Illustrated,* 2024, https://www.si.com/soccer/vinicius-junior-2024-player-of-year-real-madrid

Mugford, Simon. *Vinicius Jr Rules*. Welbeck Children's Books, 2024.

Glossary

Ballon d'Or French for Golden Ball, it is considered soccer's most prestigious individual award

Bernabéu Real Madrid's home stadium since 1947

Campeonato Brasileiro Série A
professional soccer league consisting of teams all around Brazil

Campeonato Carioca
professional soccer league of Rio de Janeiro, Brazil

Champions League premier, annual competition featuring the top clubs across Europe, determining the best team on the continent

Club World Cup annual competition featuring the best club from each continent, determining the world's best team

Copa América South America's premier international tournament contested every four years

Copa del Rey Spain's premier single-elimination cup competition featuring club teams from across the top six divisions

Copa do Brasil Brazil's premier single-elimination cup competition featuring club teams from across all regions

Copa Libertadores
premier, annual competition featuring top clubs across South America, determining the best team in the continent

Copa Sudamericana
secondary, annual competition featuring clubs across South America

derby   match between local rivals

El Clásico   match between Spanish clubs Barcelona and Real Madrid

FIFA   stands for Fédération Internationale de Football Association (French), the governing body for soccer national teams and clubs around the world

futsal   type of soccer played indoors on a hard surface. The field, ball, and team sizes are all smaller than traditional soccer.

friendly   non-competitive match without any impact on a league, tournament, or other event

La Liga   top professional soccer league of Spain

leg   one of two matches between a pair of teams

Maracanã   famous stadium in Rio De Janeiro, Brazil

Supercopa de España
four-team tournament featuring the top-performing Spanish teams

UEFA   stands for Union of European Football Associations, the governing body for European national teams and clubs

Websites

Instituto Vini Jr.
https://institutovinijr.org.br
Official website of Vini's foundation, Instituto Vini Jr.

Madrid's 'new Neymar' who feels no pressure
https://www.goal.com/story/vinicius-junior-nxgn-2018-EN/
    index.html
A closer look at Vinícius's move from Flamengo to Real Madrid

Vinicius Jr: The most important player in football
https://www.goal.com/en-us/lists/vinicius-junior-fight-against-
    racism/bltadb581cbaa456a5c
A deep dive into Vinícius's fight against racism in soccer

Vini Jr.
https://www.realmadrid.com/en-US/football/first-team/
    players/vinicius-paixao-de-oliveira-junior
Vini's official page on Real Madrid's website, filled with stats
    and more

Index

academy, 15, 17
Ancelotti, Carlo, 41, 42, 48
assists, 21, 27, 31, 2, 33, 36, 38, 39, 42, 43, 45, 47, 48, 51, 52, 53, 54, 55, 58, 60, 67, 72
awards
  Ballon d'Or, 51, 58, 70, 72, 73, 74
  Champions League Player of the Season, 67
  Champions League Young Player of the Season, 47, 67
  La Liga Team of the Season, 59
  Man of the Match, 54
  Socrates Award, 70
Brazil, 13, 15, 18, 23, 27
captain, 67
competitions
  Campeonato Brasileiro Série A, 17, 21, 27
  Campeonato Carioca, 10, 17, 18, 23, 25
  Champions League, 9, 10, 32, 35, 36, 40, 43, 47, 48, 49, 53, 57, 60, 72, 73
  Club World Cup, 33, 37, 53, 54, 68
  Copa América, 33, 41, 67, 69, 74
  Copa del Rey, 30, 35, 39, 43, 53
  Copa do Brasil, 22, 25
  Copa Libertadores, 21, 25
  Copa Sudamericana, 21, 22
  Intercontinental Cup, 68
  South American U-15 Championship, 15
  South American U-17 Championship, 17, 26
  Supercopa de España, 34
  Super Cup, 48, 72
  World Cup, 47, 51, 52, 68, 74
contract, 18, 58
controversy
  Ballon d'Or, 72–74
debut, 17, 30, 33
derbies
  El Clásico, 38, 39, 52
  Fla-Flu, 22
  Madrid derby, 30, 34
fans, 10, 40, 48, 68, 75

futsal, 14
group stage, 35, 48, 60, 67, 72
injury, 33, 57
Instituto Vini Jr., 70
knockout stage, 32, 36, 53, 60, 68, 75
professional, 17, 21, 22
Spain, 67
teammates
  Bellingham, Jude, 59, 60, 68
  Benzema, Karim, 33, 34, 43, 45, 47, 48, 53
  Kroos, Toni, 32, 39, 40
  Mbappé, Kylian, 68, 72
  Neymar, 18, 51
  Richarlison, 51
  Rodrygo, 45, 63
teams
  Brazilian national team, 17, 20, 26, 33, 41, 47, 51, 52, 67, 68, 74, 75
  Flamengo, 10, 13–27, 48, 74
trophy, 13, 22, 37, 41, 53, 59, 67, 68, 75
transfer, 18
youth, 13, 14, 15, 17